Conventions
To avoid repetition, church names are shortened, for example:
The church of St Michael, Beccles becomes St Michael's, Beccles.

Acknowledgement
Thanks are due to Elaine Blake for her help in commenting on my drafts of the text.

First published in Great Britain in 2010

British Library Cataloguing-in-Publication Data
A CIP record for this title is available from the British Library

ISBN 978 1 84114 869 4

HALSGROVE
Halsgrove House,
Ryelands Industrial Estate,
Bagley Road, Wellington, Somerset TA21 9PZ
Tel: 01823 653777   Fax: 01823 216796
email: sales@halsgrove.com

Part of the Halsgrove group of companies.
Information on all Halsgrove titles is available at: www.halsgrove.com

Printed and bound in India on behalf of JFDi Print Services Ltd

Introduction

Straddling the boundary between Norfolk and Suffolk, the Waveney Valley is one of lowland England's treasures. From the source of the River Waveney, near the timeless Redgrave and Lopham Fen, to its confluence with the River Yare below historic Burgh Castle, the river winds its way through an agricultural landscape of great antiquity. Along its meandering course, magnificent churches and timber-framed buildings peep through trees or punctuate a horizon of wide skies, marking settlements and farmsteads.

The world of the Waveney moves slowly. With the delightful market towns of Diss, Harleston, Bungay, and Beccles and several fine museums, this is an ideal place to foster low-key tourism in harmony with the environment – a point not lost on local councils as they seek to support the local economy, without spoiling the very things on which sustainable uses depend.

While the river provides the thread to this photographic journey, it is the churches, or to be more precise their towers, which clearly mark each of the parishes through which the Waveney flows.

Historic churches are this Country's greatest heritage asset, providing cultural links with the past and an expression of the endeavours and skills of those in the communities who built, looked after and used them. They are potent connections to our ancestors, as well as offering the visitor an 'I-Spy' guide to the different ways to construct a tower. When you look closely at them, you will readily see what I mean.

Ancient church buildings bring a comforting sense of continuity to the landscape, but that should not be taken for granted. Caring for their ageing structures is one of the greatest challenges facing the future of our heritage. And for that reason alone they, perhaps more than anything, deserve our fullest attention and support.

In this downstream journey I have used a small selection of the churches as touchstones to parishes adjacent to the river; there are far too many to have included them all. Not only do they provide dramatic guideposts, but also offer the best of reasons to enjoy the delightful nooks and crannies of the Norfolk and Suffolk lanes and villages, as you seek them out.

I hope that *Portrait of the Waveney Valley* will encourage everyone to linger a while, slow the pace of life and appreciate one of England's rural delights; and for those who are lucky enough to live here, that it will act as a celebration and reminder of a lovely, friendly and welcoming place.

Ian Carstairs
Harleston
Autumn 2009

Map of the area

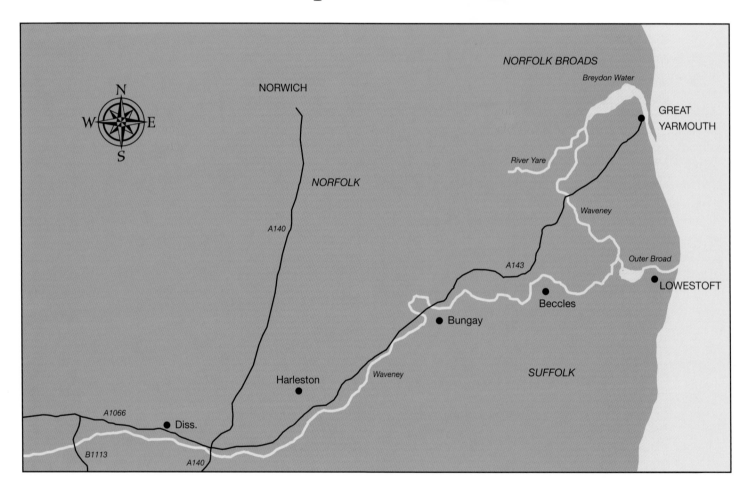

Suitable symbol
If the Waveney Valley needs a natural emblem, it should surely be the yellow water lily,
which flowers in abundance along the Upper River Waveney's course throughout the summer months.

Dividing line
Like many rivers, the Waveney defines an administrative boundary – between Norfolk and Suffolk – for most of its length. It rises in a muddy patch on the east side of the Redgrave to South Lopham Road.

Woodland start
The first few hundred metres are no more than a wet woodland ditch, seen in the
bottom right corner, where the river begins to gather water from the surrounding land.

River trail
The Angles Way UK long-distance trail from near Thetford to
Great Yarmouth follows the Waveney Valley. It first meets the river at
Redgrave and Lopham Fen, an internationally important, and spectacular,
National Nature Reserve owned by the Suffolk Wildlife Trust.

Largest left
Redgrave and Lopham Fen, the largest remaining area of river valley fen in England, is best known as a home to the rare great raft spider. The size and wildness of the Fen offers a wonderful release from the pressures of the world.

Left:
Wings of summer
Butterflies and moths have
fared badly in recent years,
because of climatic conditions
and habitat loss. Redgrave
and Lopham Fen is a
sanctuary for many species,
such as a garden tiger moth.

Opposite page:
Constant work
Maintaining the Fen requires
continuous attention and
management by professional
staff and volunteers. Left to
its own devices it would
eventually fill itself in and
turn to wet woodland, to the
detriment of its wild plants
and animals.

Munching mouths
Suffolk Wildlife Trust uses Polish Konic ponies and cattle and sheep to keep encroaching
vegetation at bay. There is a fine visitor building, picnic area and a variety of trails.

Powerful symbol – expensive exercise
St Andrew's, South Lopham, has the largest Norman church tower in the region. The building works
to the west end remind us that keeping these complex historical buildings in good order is a major and costly task.

Above:

Timely rebuild?

Many churches, such as St Remigius', Roydon, were rebuilt in the nineteenth century. A Victorian octangular top has been added to the Norman tower. What condition would it have been in without their work?

Left:

Shallow valley – wide skies

Compared with dramatic scenery and valleys of northern England, the Waveney Valley viewed from Roydon, seems but a slight depression in a gently rolling landscape, topped with a wide skyscape.

Common past and present
Wortham Ling, a lowland heath, provides a glimpse of the landscapes of the past. Managed
by The Suffolk Wildlife Trust, its mix of habitats is home to a wide variety of wildlife.

Largest known
Said to be the largest round church tower in the
Country, the ruined remains sit slightly bizarrely with
the diminutive weather-vane-topped wooden
bell-cote of St Mary's, Wortham.

Nothing is forever
The Chequers Inn, Bressingham, an evocative building on the main road along the Waveney Valley, welcomed travellers for centuries, until shortly after this photograph was taken. In October 2009 it was completely destroyed by fire.

Pure nostalgia
Four generations of a family ride the smallest of the railway experiences at Bressingham Steam Museum, as the 'Three o'clock' heads round the gardens created by world-renowned horticulturalist Alan Bloom.

19

What goes round, comes round
Bressingham's famous Victorian Steam 'Gallopers' carousel ride, with the organ's
inimitable music, is a colourful favourite with visitors to the museum.

Commanding presence
St John the Baptist's, Bressingham has a picture-perfect presence, especially when you approach along the Thetford to Diss Road.

Not plain at all
A magnificent plane tree defines the streetscape in Palgrave where cottages and houses front a wide green.

At the heart
Palgrave, with its mix of building styles, spreads widely
– St Peter's, is at its centre. A fine timber-framed
building with first floor 'jettied' (protruding out) over
the ground floor stands opposite the church.

Gateway
The market town of Diss lies at a communications cross roads, with main roads connecting to Bury St Edmunds, Great Yarmouth, Ipswich and Norwich and a main railway line to Norwich and London.

Top of the town
Standing on high ground at the head of the town, St Mary's perfectly caps Diss Market Place on a beautiful autumn day.

Time-honoured role
Dolphin House, will have
always been an important
building in Diss' street scene.
It might once have been a
wool merchant's house and
was later a public house,
before becoming home to a
number of small businesses.

Postal confidence
With such a grand historic neighbour as Dolphin House, the bold character of Diss Post Office, can easily be overlooked.

Making the most of the past
Diss Museum is based in a building known as The Shambles – a name possibly derived from 'shammels',
the sturdy shelves used to display meat; the building once housed two butchers' shops.

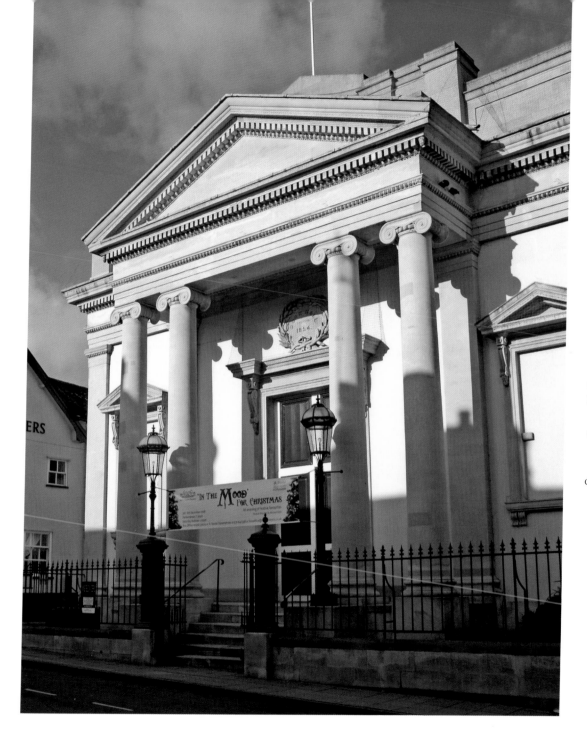

Rome comes to rural Norfolk . . .
Classical-style buildings were quite the fashion in nineteenth century England. Diss Corn Hall's agricultural role has long gone and today it is an entertainments venue. The cost of maintaining it is a serious challenge for the community.

. . . and round the corner too This well-maintained façade demonstrates that protecting our heritage is always easier when buildings have a clear economically valuable use – 2 Mount Street is a solicitors' office.

Street gathering

Diss tourist information centre 'attracts' a queue of street furniture – litter bin, street light, road signs, post box, telephone box, and several bollards – they will give people who look at this photograph in the future insights into how we do things.

Deep time
At 18 feet deep – with another 51 feet of mud below – Diss Mere is one of the deeper natural lakes in the Country.

Delicate spray
Diss Rotary Club presented a fountain to the town as an attractive feature to celebrate the organisation's 100th anniversary.

Moving story
A large erratic granite boulder moved by the forces of the ice sheets thousands of years ago,
has been on the move again, to the middle of a roundabout in a main supermarket.

Winged wood
An intricately carved corner-post on a centuries-old timber-framed building at the southern end of
Diss Market Place, confirms the durability of oak as a building material.

Enduring traditions
Shoppers queue for chips on Market Day, outside Dolphin House, Diss – a quintessentially British tradition.

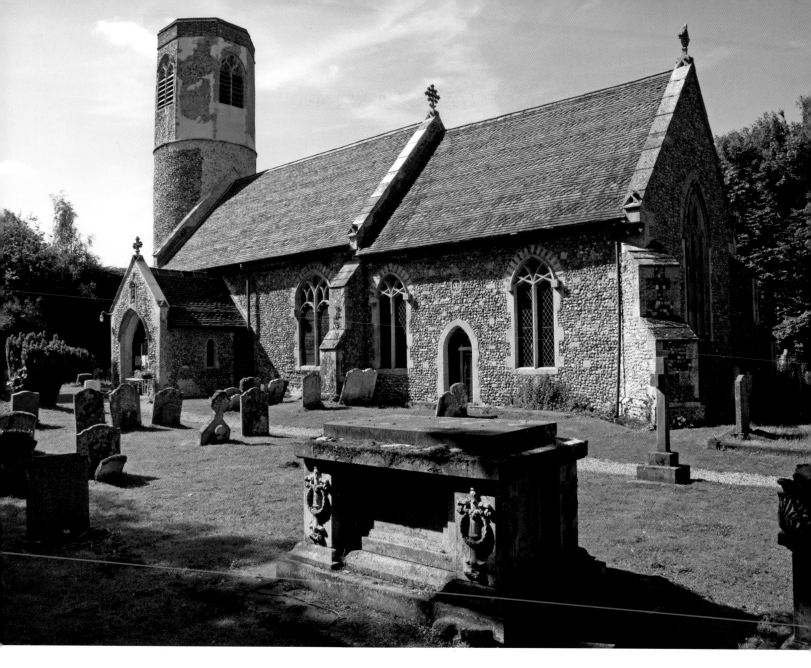

Tucked away
Surrounded by trees, even a relatively large building can prove quite hard to find. In many churchyards,
trees and vegetation, like at All Saints', Stuston are a haven for birds and other wildlife.

'Crabbing' up. . .
Great spotted woodpeckers are frequently heard (a distinctive sharp 'tchackk'), and sometimes seen,
working their way up and round tree-trunks in search of food, or drumming on a dead limb in spring

Creeping down
Nuthatches are the only birds in Britain,
which regularly make a habit of
coming head-first down trees.

Widening way

Below Diss, the Waveney's floodplain opens out. The field patterns of these grasslands have avoided major agricultural change. They are still used for what they do best – growing grass for livestock.

Evening calm
Late autumn light etches tranquillity across the isolated St Nicholas' churchyard, Oakley.

Place in history
Hoxne has more than its share
of history: the Hoxne hoard of
Roman coins, and other artefacts
was discovered in 1992;
St Edmund is said to have
been martyred here, and
archaeological discoveries gave
rise to naming the Hoxnian
Interglacial period.

Old haunt

The Scole Inn, a seventeenth century coaching Inn, stands at the junction between the old Ipswich to Norwich, and Bury St Edmunds to Great Yarmouth roads (now by-passed). Guests are said to have included Charles II and Nelson.

That which burns can return

St Andrew's, Scole was badly damaged by fire in the early 1960s. Rebuilt, it now forms part of a four-churches grouping, with Brockdish, Thorpe Abbotts and Billingford, which hold joint events from time to time.

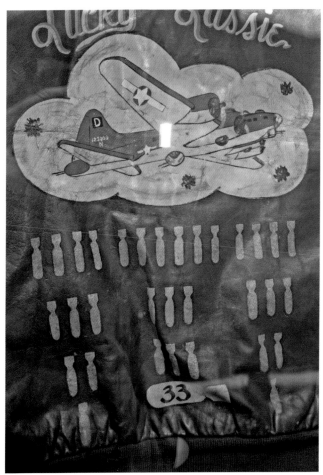

Sobering thoughts
Dedicated to the United States Air Force's 'Bloody 100th' Bomb Group,
Thorpe Abbotts' Museum, portrays the daily life of this
Second World War bomber base. Details on a flying jacket bring
home the enormity of events played out in the past.

Stars and Stripes
The United States flag flies over
the 100th Bomb Group
Museum's memorial to General
Curtis E. Lemay (1906 –1990)
Commander 3rd Air Division,
8th Air Force, World War II.

Tucked against the trees
The squat truncated tower with its tile 'hat' gives the pretty St Leonard's, Billingford, an unusual appearance.

Above:
One of many
Norfolk is said to have one of the highest densities of mediaeval churches in the world.
All Saints', Thorpe Abbotts sits beside the A143 Road, some way from its
village. The word *Thorpe*, suggests Viking connections with the settlement.

Left:
Pastoral scene
Billlingford, as its name suggests, denotes a historic crossing place of
the River Waveney. Today a narrow bridge spans the river giving a romantic
view over cattle grazing in the riverside pastures late on a summer's evening.

Above:
Making a mark
St Peter and St Paul's, Brockdish embraces the skills of craftsmen spanning
our recorded history from the first building in Saxon times through to
inclusion of a distinctive stair turret in the nineteenth century.

Left:
Wind – a force for good and ill
Wind power ground the corn, but it also blew down Billingford Mill's predecessor in 1859.
This was the last mill to be operated commercially by wind in Norfolk.

Breadbasket
As the ground rises above the Waveney's floodplain, arable agriculture dominates the land use.

Plenty around
Of 185 round-towered churches known in England,
162 are in Norfolk and Suffolk, with a good number,
including St Peter's, Needham, found along the
Waveney Valley.

Room for expansion
After heavy rains in its catchement, the River Waveney, unconstrained by the straightjacket of floodbanks,
rises quickly to spread across its floodplain at Shotford Bridge near Harleston.

Pivotal point

Harleston clock tower is a 'beacon' for the surrounding communities. The top of the tower is formed from the cupola of the chapel, demolished beside where the clock tower now stands in 1873.

Miniscule museum
The endearing Harleston Museum must
rate among the smallest in the Country.
Committed volunteers from the Harleston and
District Historical Society create all
its displays about local life.

Old town
Harleston, a traditional market town, retains an enviable range of independent shops. Unlike other towns
along the Valley it has never suffered a catastrophic fire, so nearly all the properties are historic listed buildings.

Little . . .
Tiny, Orkney Cottage, in Broad Street, Harleston is a
significant benchmark in the history of buildings. It was
built in the spring of 1769, the latest known date for
this type of building in Norfolk.

. . . and large
Dating from the early 1600s The Swan Hotel, a former Coaching Inn, is Harleston's largest historic timber-framed building. As fashions changed, the Georgians added an imposing brick front.

Above:

Community support

Events to raise funds for Cancer research have seen more than 90 decorated
tractors driven by women parading through the streets and between villages.
Each run has raised a large sum of money.

Left:

Mist and shadows

Daybreak in spring over Ocean Pit, Weybread, one of the
large bodies of water created through gravel extraction.

The year turns
A dramatic sunrise over Ocean Pit, Weybread, heralds the beginning of the shortest day of the year.

Night-light
A phenomenon known as noctiluscent (night shining) clouds casts an eerie
electric-blue light across a mid-summer sky over Harleston at dusk.

Above:
Power provider
The waters of the River Waveney once powered numerous mills.
At Weybread, the mill was destroyed in a fierce blaze in February 1920.
Today only a sluice marks where the mill once stood.

Left:
Winter's trail
A light fall of snow defines the River Waveney
near the old road to Shotford from Needham.

Wonderful wood
This oak tree near Needham has been cut off at some time in the past resulting in multi-stems rather than a single continuous trunk.

A hero remembered
The frequency of round towers in Norfolk reflects the local geology and predominance of flint as a building material. Suffolk's first Victoria Cross winner, Alfred Ablett, is commemorated on a plaque in St Andrew's, Weybread.

Above:
Sign of the times
The massive St Mary's, Redenhall tower, is a product of the area's
wealth, when wool drove the economy of this region.

Right:
Wide skies
From Cuckoo Hill, between Harleston and Mendham, the arable lands slope
down to the wide floodplain of the River Waveney. At night, with very
little light pollution, spectacular views of the stars can be gained.

Time warp
Ignore the modern agricultural building and tarmac road and it could be any time in the last 400 years,
except that this thatched-cottage in Withersdale is now nicely painted and carefully maintained.

Lazy river
For much of its course, the slow-flowing River Waveney lies high within its banks, such as below Mendham Bridge.

Famous painter
Thatch cottages are plentiful in East Anglia where reeds provide a source of roofing materials. Sir Alfred Munnings, renowned painter of horses, lived in Mendham, whose public house on the right bears his name.

Autumn in England
All Saints', Mendham with its fourteenth century tower was restored in the late 1800s.
Flint is extensively used, with stone corners to give strength to the structure of the building.

Life after death
Churchyards are some of the most undisturbed places for wildlife. They still need
management to keep them at their best for plants and animals while respecting those who lie at rest.

Poor visibility – pure silence
Grazing cattle add to the magic of the landscape on an early summer morning by the River Waveney, near Mendham.
The mist not only limits vision, but also wonderfully blots out the sound of distant traffic.

A fine day to come
The sun bursts through woodland near Wortwell, burning off the mist ahead of a beautiful day to come.

The village awakes
Poles, wires, light and post box, are all part of a twenty-first century street scene,
with a couple of Wortwell's Muscovy ducks for good measure.

First signs
Autumn begins to tinge an English oak. The Waveney Valley and its
surrounding parishes are remarkably full of trees and hedges.

In the red
Overgrown hedges in Denton show off an abundance of colourful fruits as the season moves on.
Clockwise from top left: bittersweet, wild rose, hawthorn and black bryony.

Ancient hedges
Many hedgerows are very old and can be broadly dated by the range of species they contain –
clockwise from the top left: crab apple, hawthorn and field maple grow next to each other.

80

Blaze of colour
Little surpasses
the brassy glow of
a woodland beech
tree growing
alongside the
Angles Way near
Homersfield.

After high water
The swollen River Waveney shrinks back into its banks after a flood has passed.
St Mary's, Homersfield tower peeps over the nearby woods.

Earliest of its kind
Built for the Flixton Estate in 1869, Homersfield Bridge is the oldest concrete bridge in Britain. The Arms of the Adair family are displayed on both sides. The Norfolk Historic Buildings Trust restored the bridge in 1995.

Double-take
The Norfolk and Suffolk Aviation Museum, Flixton takes you completely by surprise. Behind a pub are gathered a collection of aircraft with dramatic names including Meteor, Lightning, Super Sabre, Javelin and this French, Dassault Mystere.

Unpleasant memories
An insect-like Argentinean Pucara, relic of the Falklands War, is an unusual reminder of difficult times.

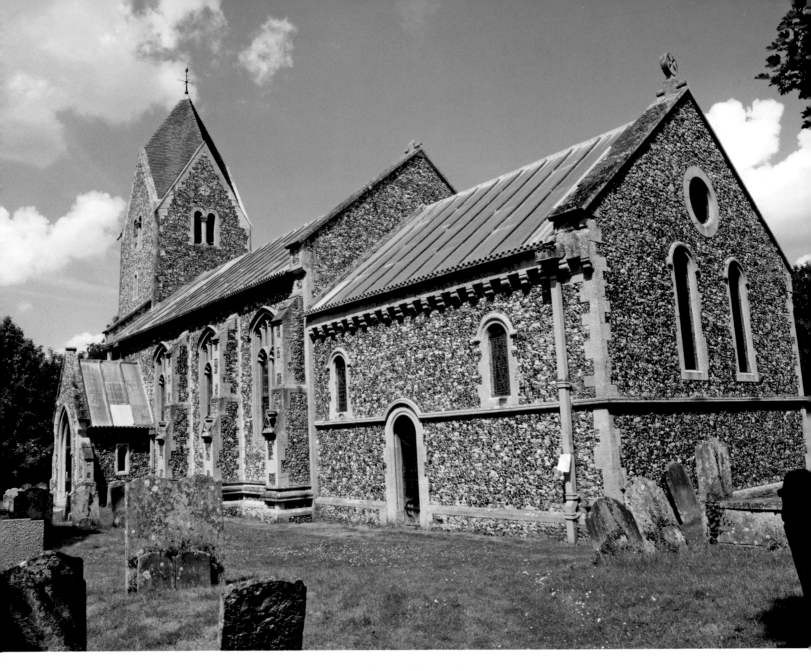

Lavish flintwork
Major restoration of St Mary's, Flixton in the mid 1800s, saw the earlier Saxon tower,
which had collapsed, rebuilt in a highly distinctive form.

Idyllic setting

All Saints', Alburgh lies well to the east of this straggling village. Among its historic features are two fifteenth century benches with poppy heads on their ends. The churchyard is well-managed to help wildlife.

Piecemeal construction
Close examination of St Mary's, Denton reveals various stages of modification and additions in the evolution of the tower.

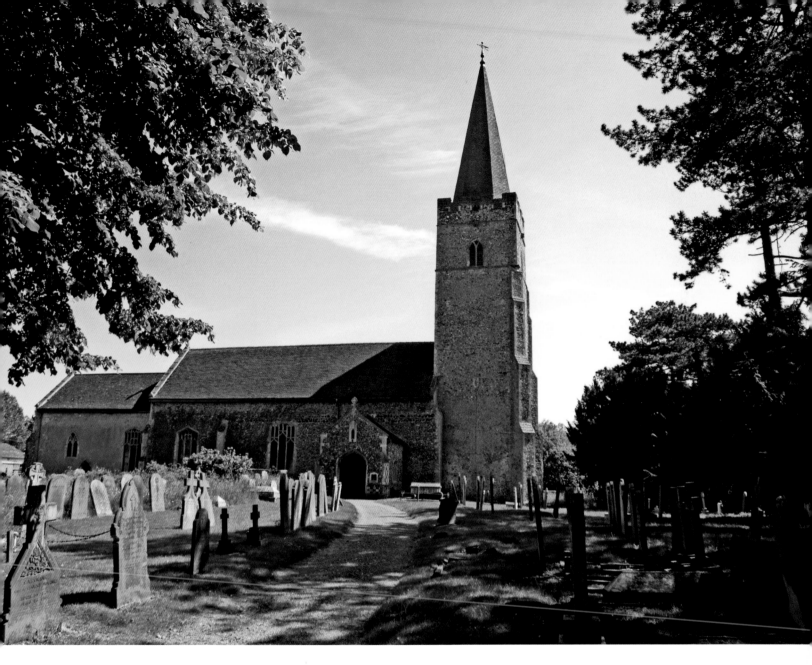

Pointed presence
Unusually for the area, All Saints', Earsham, sports a spire. Places with names such as Earsham,
ending in – *ham* are Anglian in origin, named before the arrival of the Vikings in the ninth century.

Above:
Saving a favourite
Following the severe decline of the otter from the 1960s, the Otter Trust,
based in Earsham, spearheaded its comeback. Today otter numbers
are recovering and the Trust's mission has been accomplished – fantastic!

Right:
Road view
The view in high summer from the A143 road bridge across the River Waveney,
where the river partly encircles the town of Bungay, is reminiscent of
the romantic style of nineteenth century landscape painters.

Past in the present
Established in 1963, Bungay Museum is housed above
Waveney District Council's offices in an attractively
decorated building. Local people have created and
contributed to the collections.

Day sadly done
The now redundant, St Mary's, Bungay, a focal point of the town and surrounding landscape, is looked after by the Churches Conservation Trust and supported by a Friends organisation.

Early foundation
The ruins of a Bendictine Priory lie adjacent to St Mary's Church. Gundreda,
wife of Roger Bigod, the First Earl of Norfolk, founded the Priory in 1160.

Keeping it up

Ruins need maintenance to stop them from falling down.
Bungay Castle was erected by Roger Bigod, in the early
twelfth century, rebuilt in the thirteenth century
and said to have been old and ruinous by 1382.

Fire – a force to be reckoned with
In 1688 Bungay suffered a devastating fire, which destroyed its town centre.
Much of the street-scene today results from the re-building of that era.

Selling across the centuries
Rebuilt after the town fire, the Grade 1 listed historic Buttercross (market cross),
lies in the market place where a weekly market has been held since 1382.

Crime and punishment
A fine – if that's the right word – example of whipping post irons,
used to restrain offenders, on one of the pillars of the Buttercross.

Proper shops
Small independent shops in each of the Waveney Valley's market towns are treasured by
residents and visitors alike. Without them the heart of the communities would be lost.

Above:
Out in the open
Like Ditchingham Parish Church (opposite),
St Michael's, Broome, stands isolated in open countryside.
Why was it built in what now seems such a remote location?

Left:
Far apart
St Mary's, Ditchingham stands well away from its village,
lending an ethereal quality to the landscape.

Wet wonderland
The riverside marshes, meadows and pastures along the Waveney Valley, such as at Ellingham,
offer ideal breeding and wintering grounds for wildfowl and wading birds.

Swan-upping
The Waveney Valley is renowned for the large numbers of mute swans, which make it home.

No longer turning
Of the numerous
historic watermills
along the Waveney,
only Ellingham, seen
here, and Earsham are
on the Norfolk side of
the river. The mill was
built on an artificial
cut. It ceased milling
in the mid twentieth
century.

Attractive legacy
The cut, returning the millstream to the river, is a lovely place for leaning on the railings
and contemplating the activity when the mill played a part in the commercial life of the area.

Above:
Home in the hedge
High and wide hedgerows are vital corridors for wildlife. Hedges need to be cut back from time to time, otherwise they become too tall, shade themselves out, and lose their value.

Left
Taking trade upstream
In 1670 an Act of Parliament was passed to improve the navigation on the Waveney between Beccles and Bungay. This part of the statutory navigation was closed in 1934 and the lock subsequently converted to a sluice.

Tree-nester
Sometimes known by the local name 'hansa', the grey heron is a common sight standing in the river and ditches or flying with deep wing-beats over the Valley.

Wild by the wheels
Roadside verges are extensive 'nature reserves'. Sometimes they host a spectacular show of
wildflowers, like this short stretch of verge near Shipmeadow, where dozens of Pyramidal orchids flourish.

Long history
What a relief to see a
historic building –
Mettingham Castle –
quietly getting on with
being part of an
everyday unorganised
scene: no visitor
centre, no commercial
signs, in fact no
access either.

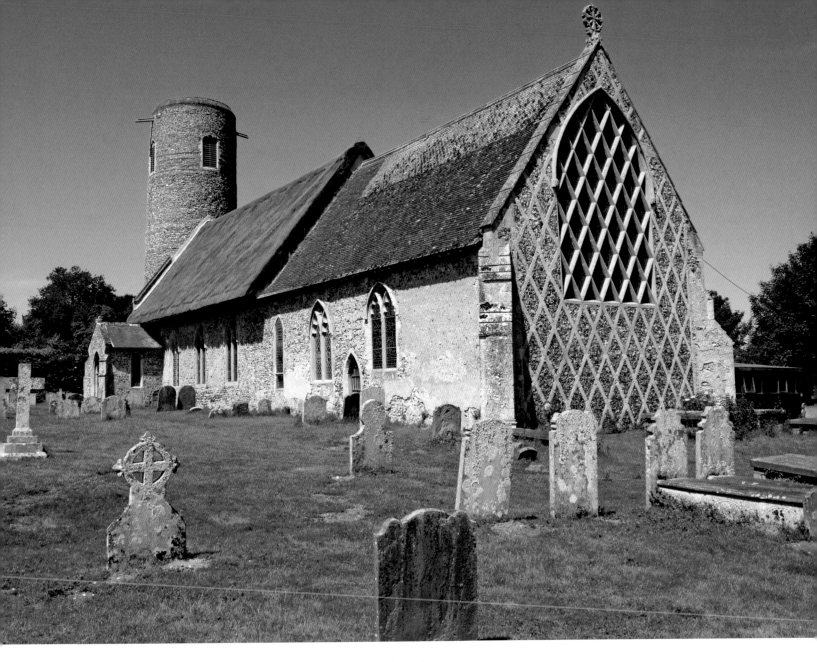

Diamonds set in stone

Walking to the east end of Holy Trinity, Barsham, brings quite a surprise: a complex
lattice work and diamond pattern of flint covers the whole of the end of the building.

A gem
Tucked among trees, St Michael's, Geldestone, can be easily missed. The cockerel symbol that is
seen on so many church weather vanes symbolises Peter's denial of Christ, thrice, before the cock crowed.

Stand alone
In 1584 Queen Elizabeth I granted Beccles a Charter under
which it was run until 1835. Beccles' eighteenth-century Town
Hall stands on the site of the original medieval market cross.
St Michael's tower, behind, was built separately from its church.

Classic role
Standing on the site of the churchyard of St Peters' Church, the eighteenth century
St Peter's House exerts a powerful presence over Old Market, Beccles.

Painted 'plaster'

A pretty example of an old timber-framed building with jettied first floor complements the character of Old Market. The bollards are needed to keep the pavements clear of vehicles – a pity, but necessary.

Centre for leisure

The Lower Waveney forms part of the Broads 'National Park'. In earlier times Beccles was a centre for river trade, but today, The Quay is used for recreational enjoyment of the waterway.

Tourist trip
A river trip boat sets out from Beccles Quay so that passengers can enjoy the River Waveney and its landscape.

International effect
A repainted advertisement on a brick 'Dutch' gable – a reminder of the influences from our neighbours across the North Sea – tells that "wherries [cargo sailing vessels] constantly attend the traders . . . from the wharf".

STAITHE
SMITH & EASTAUGH
CORN & COAL MERCHANTS.
Dealers in Malt & Hops of the best quality.
BEANS. PEAS. OATS. POLLARD. CINDERS
WHOLESALE & RETAIL
Wherries constantly attend the Traders & Steam Vessels for conveying goods to and from the wharf.

Lazy days
Beccles waterfront is an ideal place for a leisurely walk, or to take to the river – muscle-power is the order of the day on this boating trip.

Above:

Seat of learning

Leman House (c.1570), once the Grammar School, was modernised in the 1760s. Today it houses the Beccles Museum.
Its beautiful façade is rarely seen without a line of parked cars, but that is the reality of our time.

Right:

Gardener's delight

The steep slope from the town to the river encourages imaginative use of space for
domestic gardens and enables glimpses of the individual gardener's handiwork.

March through time

Beccles Marsh Trail offers a chance to enjoy the sights and sounds of the countryside alongside the river. A somewhat obtrusive, but nonetheless useful, information panel tells of the Bronze Age trackway found running alongside the path.

Broads cruising
The advent of foreign holidays caused a decline in the number of visitors to the Norfolk Broads over the years. But the economic downturn might see local fortunes improving. Will it last?

Over the edge
An iconic 'Union Jack' Mini, below the wall and cliff edge at the end of St Michael's churchyard, Beccles.

Norman by design
The robust pattern of a Norman-arched west doorway greets the visitor at
St Mary's, Aldeby. Settlement names ending in *-by* are of Viking origin.

Above:
All square
The Tudors left us one of the most attractive church towers
along the Waveney Valley. At All Saints', Wheatacre, the tower is faced
with a chequer pattern formed from red brick and panels of flint.

Right:
Misty moment
Fog rolls eerily across the remote marshes near Burgh St Peter.

Stepping-up
The extraordinary St Mary's, Burgh St Peter looks more like a Ziggurat (stepped-pyramid) than a rural English parish church tower.

Ticket to ride
Blackpool Corporation and Amsterdam trams line up for rides, to be followed by a nice cup of tea
at the East Anglia Transport Museum, at Carlton Colville.

Bendy-brick
Wavy 'crinkle-crankle' walls provide greater strength as well as sheltered places to grow fruit by catching the sun and lessening the effect of wind. This example in Carlton Colville is a historic listed building.

Short cut
Oulton Dyke, links the River Waveney with Oulton Broad, a popular tourist location. From here,
boats pass through Mutford Lock into Lake Lothing and then can sail on to Lowestoft and out to sea.

Modern mess
Oulton Broad, is known as the 'southern gateway to the Broads'. A myriad contraptions, lights and signs, festoon the area where swing road and railway bridges, a lifting footbridge and boats passing through Mutford Lock meet.

The way to do it
Somerleyton's planned mid-nineteenth-century
'model' village has a unique character, highlighted
by the delightful primary school.

Left: The village shop was voted the UK's
best Community Post Office of the year in 2009.

Above:
Quality throughout
Laburnums in the churchyard frame the fifteenth century tower of St Mary's, Somerleyton.
The effect of the Somerleyton country estate gives a well-kept air to its surroundings.

Right:
Weather in the west
Looking across Haddiscoe marshes from the Great Yarmouth Road. Two extra-tall pylons
carry overhead electricity cables across the New Cut between Thurlton and Fritton Marshes.

From sea to city
Haddiscoe Cut, also known as the New Cut, opened in 1833, provides a more direct route between Lowestoft and Norwich.
Prior to that boats had to travel further downstream on the River Waveney and back up the River Yare.

Single span
St. Olave's mini Tyne or Sydney Harbour bridge, predates both by more than 70 years.
Built in 1847 to replace a sixteenth century stone bridge, it is a historic listed building.

Rare ruins
The ruins of St Olave's, an Augustinian Priory, include a rare example of early brickwork, forming the undercroft. Founded in 1213, it commemorates an eleventh-century King of Norway.

Piggy-back pill box
Full marks for improvisation – a World War I defensive pill-box, has been high-jacked
as a base for a small office in a boatyard alongside St Olave's Bridge.

Calling time

The Bell Inn, St Olave's, a late sixteenth-century building, is reputed to be the oldest public house in the Norfolk Broads.

Robust remains
A bastion and walls at Burgh Castle, a Roman fort (c.270 AD) testify to the strength of Roman construction techniques. Two young 'jokers' enjoy lending a hand to keep our heritage standing.

Ready supply
Built shortly after the Norman Conquest in 1066, St Paul's, Burgh Castle, undoubtedly
incorporates materials from the Roman fort, including pieces of Roman Brick.

Temporary land?
In Roman times, Burgh Castle Fort stood over a wide estuary, with a wharf below the Castle. Reclamation
and drainage have created and maintained the marshes . . . but in a low-lying area, for how much longer?

Crushing climax
The Berney Arms windmill (c.1870), originally built for crushing cement,
makes a perfect 'full stop' to our journey. From here the Waveney's waters join
those of the River Yare, pass through Breydon Water, then out into the North Sea.